THE
# RUNNING DOGS
# OF LOYALTY

# THE
# RUNNING DOGS
# OF LOYALTY:

## Honest Reflections
## on a Magical Zoo

—for those over 30 only—

Go to the fair an' see the funny fowls,
The double-headed pigeon an' the one-eyed owl;
The ol' lame goose with a web 'tween 'er toes
She laughs 'erself to death w'en the shanghi crows...

—James Ball Naylor
*Ralph Marlowe*
1901, p. 44

## Gale Richard Walker

GATEWAY PRESS, INC.
Baltimore, MD     1995

This book may be purchased by check or money order by writing:
BookCrafters, Inc.
615 East Industrial Drive
Chelsea, MI 48118

or by credit card by calling

1-800-879-4214

Price: $9.95 plus $4.50 for shipping and handling.
Please make checks payable to BookCrafters.

Library of Congress Catalog Card Number 95-78232
ISBN 0-9647972-0-8

Cover design and art by Bruce Rydell

Published for the author by
Gateway Press, Inc.
1001 N. Calvert Street
Baltimore, MD 21202

Printed in the United States of America

Dedicated to

**Dirk H. van der Elst**

the first free-thinker I ever met and to

**Leon Bailey**

one of the deepest free-thinkers I ever met.

# Table of Contents

Chapter One

# The Meeting

---

"You sons of bitches, the zoo is not right," said Top Baboon to the others assembled in the room. His voice was smooth. He was well groomed. "There must be more efficiency, more happiness, more dedication. Team work in the days ahead will..."

Sly Fox leaned to his side and whispered in the ear of Gray Fox next to him, "Another reorganization of the cages. Wonder who will get mounted in the rear this time." Gray Fox grinned with a wince.

"The outworld is filled with Jackals and Wolves," Top Baboon continued. "They would devour us if they could. You are lucky we high ranking Baboons are here to lead you. Otherwise you would be eaten alive."

Whenever Top Baboon invoked the outworld Jackal Principle, the hop-to-it Rabbits in the room became nervous. Of course, the hop-to-it Rabbits were always nervous. While Top Baboon spoke, worker Ants moved silently among the others, distributing packets of charts and graphs. The silent Ants were skilled at being present, but invisible.

"You should appreciate the cages we have given you. You should be proud to be in this Zoo. Nothing less than your full dedication and loyalty will see us succeed," said Top Baboon in his usual pep-talk tone. Then in a grave voice he said, "Together, with teamwork, we will succeed in the competition against the outworld Jackals. But to do this, we must have better lines of communication. To facilitate our more efficient..."

"Here it comes," thought Sly Fox. The Barking Seals and Running Dogs of Loyalty in attendance all sat at attention. Of course, Barking Seals and Running Dogs of Loyalty always sat at attention when Top Baboon spoke. The old Sloths in the back sat expressionless. Of course, the old Sloths always sat expressionless.

"...and efficacious use of our various talents and precious resources, after thorough review, it has been decided that several departments will be reorganized and the smaller cages consolidated as outlined in the chart presented by ranking Baboon No. 2. We trust you all have had ample..."

A pension Barnacle seated in the corner thought to himself, "This is my fifth Top Baboon. If I could suffer the others, I can survive this one, too. He sounds like all the rest—concocting improved means to unimproved ends.[1] Holy Lions! Of course the zoo is not right. The zoo is *never* right. Does he think this is news!"

"...and I want you all to know that as long as I'm Top Baboon there will be no Rats, Skunks, Weasels, or Moles tolerated in this organization."

The Running Dogs of Loyalty all smiled and nodded in agreement. A Running Dog of Loyalty hates an unruly Skunk.

Continued Top Baboon, "...quarterly reports show

good improvement in some areas. Night noise is down considerably in the Bird Division. They are to be congratulated. In other divisions more attention will have to be given to cage cleanliness. Especially in the Primate Division. Appearances are important. As you know, we take our motto seriously: To groom is to bloom. I'm sure you will be looking forward to our new projects and..."

Thought Sly Fox, "Really sick."

When Top Baboon finished his address, the Barking Seals all clapped. Of course, Barking Seals always applauded whatever Top Baboon said. They were joined by the Running Dogs of Loyalty and, of course, the ranking Baboons.

Sly Fox said to Gray Fox, "The louder he speaks of his honor, the faster I check for Fleas."

Chapter Two

## After the Meeting

---

In late afternoon in a cage in Zooland two Foxes talked with a Young Pup. "Aren't the new projects and initiatives that Top Baboon outlined exciting!" gushed Young Pup.

Gray Fox glanced at Sly Fox. After an awkward silence, he said to Sly Fox, "Let's take a chance and tell him, shall we?"

"Okay," said Sly Fox critically, "But it won't do any good. Over the years I've seen Young Pups come here by the score. There is no way you can teach them. They are too eager. They have to learn the hard way, by themselves. They have to be mounted, you know."

Gray Fox, with kindness in his voice, said, "This Pup here, though, is pretty bright. Besides, I like him. He was one of the better Pups in Young Pup School. He went to the same Young Pup School I did. He drank from the dish of free thinking. I assure you his brain is not yet lie-locked."

Sly Fox glanced away, looking pensively at the ceiling of the cage, then said, "The learning of many things does not teach understanding.[2] But go ahead. Give it a try. Maybe someday he will understand. Maybe someday, when we are pension Barnacles, he will remember us kindly. But I warn you. You can't make a sly Fox out of a Young Pup in a day."

"That is true," answered Gray Fox, "but one can begin." Turning to Young Pup, Gray Fox said, "One of the wisest Foxes who ever lived said, 'The time comes when each one of us has to give up as illusions the expectations which, in his youth, he pinned upon his fellow creatures, and when he may learn how much difficulty and pain has been added to his life by their ill-will.'[3] These wise words you cannot understand. Yet, they may be a warning to you that..."

Suddenly from a cage nearby came the doleful cry of a Persian poet Parrot:

With them the Seed of Wisdom did I sow,
And with my own hand labour'd it to grow:
   And this was all the Harvest that I reap'd—
I came like water, and like Wind I go."

Sly Fox fumed, "Those damn Birds. Always interrupting. Unpredictably, too. Which wouldn't be so bad if you could talk with them. But they simply cry out, then fall silent. That one is always reciting some ancient, awkward rhyme. He seems to think he is some sort of artist—as if art could have meaning under conditions of meaninglessness!" Sly Fox went over to the bars of the cage and yelled, "Hey, you Bird. Be quiet! We are trying to have an intelligent conversation over here. So shut up!" Turning back to the others he said, "Won't do any good. Never does."

Gray Fox said, "A few think the Parrot is a genius. Most simply ignore him. He is as rare as he is odd.

Nothing you can do except listen to him." Turning to Young Pup, Gray Fox said, "Young Pup, you are new here to the zoo. There are things which you do not perceive. You do not understand the nature of this zoo or the kinds of creatures who inhabit it. From your naivete you think others are like yourself. You think they think like you. You do not understand the hidden meaning of the zoo rituals and the hidden messages behind what you hear. Things are not what they seem. Many words mean the opposite of what they mean. This is a magical zoo in which creatures change into one another and their cages are periodically rearranged. Yet, the zoo never changes."

Again came the mocking cry of Persian poet Parrot:

For in and out, above, about, below,
'Tis nothing but a Magic Shadow-show
   Play'd in a Box whose Candle is the Sun
Round which we Phantom Figures come and go.

Again, Sly Fox was annoyed. He yelled out, "That's twice now, Bird brain. Shut up!" Turning to the others he complained, "Sometimes this place is a real zoo."

Young Pup thought to himself that the harshness of Sly Fox's words betrayed a certain respect, if not envy, for the Bird's intelligence. Young Pup felt good inside that the Foxes would take him into their confidence, but uneasy about what they were trying to tell him. No one in Young Pup School had mentioned such bizarre possibilities. "Changing creatures?" he wondered. Despite his apprehension, the Foxes had made him feel special. Young Pup wanted to learn, so he asked them to tell him more. He listened intently.

"You must learn to beware of climbing Baboons," said Gray Fox. "There is a pecking order here. Climbing Baboons have various ranks. They occupy almost all of the upper cages. And never mind what anybody else tells you, it is a hierarchy maintained by fear. Sometimes it is subtle, as in symbolic gestures or threats, and sometimes it is overt as in screeching and screaming. Whichever, you will learn that climbing Baboons, if need be, demonstrate their superiority over others by suddenly mounting them from the rear. To be suddenly mounted from the rear by a climbing Baboon is certainly painful. If done in front of others it is very humiliating. This is how the hierarchy is established and how it is ultimately maintained. The more creatures one can mount, the higher the rank."

Young Pup thought to himself, "This can't be true." His eyes were wide with disbelief. "Has this ever happened to you?" he asked anxiously.

"Oh, yes. Quite by surprise. By a small gang of them. But only once. I learn fast," said Sly Fox licking his red fur as if licking a wound. "Fortunately climbing Baboons mostly mount each other. They seldom bother to mount a hop-to-it Rabbit and never the worker Ants."

Young Pup, upset by these thoughts, blurted out, "How about Young Pups?"

The Foxes glanced at each other, realizing they were explaining too much too fast. Gray Fox said softly, "No. Climbing Baboons never mount a Young Pup. You have nothing to worry about. The worst that ever happens to a Young Pup is that a ranking Baboon may take the time to momentarily sit on him. That always suffices."

Sly Fox added a disturbing qualifier, "...for now." He went on, "The reason the climbing Baboons don't bother to mount Young Pups, worker Ants, or seldom any other creatures is that it makes them look unnecessarily cruel and it really does not advance them. They advance themselves by mounting their rivals, not their underlings. They only mount underlings to remind them that they are underlings, and that is seldom necessary."

After a long pause to see how Young Pup was taking all this, Gray Fox said, "We tell you this for two reasons. First, you believe that the tasks and goals set forth by Top Baboon are new and exciting. Nothing is further from the truth. They are neither new nor exciting. They are old and boring. But even if they were a worthy mission, it doesn't matter. You miss the point. You were witness to an institutionalized mounting. That is the true meaning of the ritual, its hidden purpose."

"Young Pups," Sly Fox interrupted harshly, "don't understand that killing one's fellow creature is a messy, difficult affair when done openly. Victims sometimes fight back, which often makes the climbing Baboons look vicious or weak. Even stupid. One thing a climbing baboon hates worse than to appear weak is to appear stupid. A carcass makes a real stink in the zoo. Getting rid of it is not always easy. But under the guise of ritual reorganization and in the name of increasing efficiency to defeat the outworld Jackals, Top Baboons can get rid of whomever they want. Especially their rivals. Few do they really seek to outright banish from the zoo. They merely want to publicly mount them to keep them in their place. It is done in the name of the good of the zoo, of course. Top Baboons always think they know what is in the best interests of the zoo: Their's. Remember, when you hear a Top Baboon promise how good it would be for the zoo to 'bring in some fresh blood,' he wants somebody's old blood spilled on the bottom of a cage."

Gray Fox continued, "That's right. And the second reason we tell you this is for your own protection. This is a magical zoo. Creatures change. You cannot always tell what kind of creature you are talking to merely by looking him in the face. Worse, not only do they sometimes change, many are two-faced, even three-faced. They say one thing in one group, then the opposite in another. Some are particularly treacherous and deceitful. Many others just have no idea who they are. They are moral Chameleons. A shallowness of character is a symptom of our time. This is no accident. It is structured that way. As a Young Pup you are secure from mounting, but you won't be a Young Pup forever."

The sudden and obvious truth of this shook Young Pup. "What will I be?" he blurted.

"That will be up to you," said Gray Fox. "Which niche in the zoo would you like to fill? You may become a hop-to-it Rabbit. You may become a Barking Seal. You may even become a Running Dog of Zooland Loyalty or a climbing Baboon yourself. Over the years you will probably be several of these. Only time will tell. Quite likely in the end you will become a burned-out Sloth or a pension Barnacle. Most do."

Sly Fox said, "But that is jumping way ahead. We, of course, hope one day you will become a Fox. A Fox is one who not only has talent, but who also can think *critically*. You will be surprised to discover how many talented creatures cannot think for themselves. I warn you, thinking for yourself in Zooland is dangerous. You must be on your guard. Being a Fox will make you lonely. Your friends will be few. Your tongue will be censored. The Fox lives on the margins, by his wits. The Fox is in the zoo, but not of it. He maintains a healthy alienation from his role. His only den of rest is his own mind."

"I don't think I comprehend much of what you are telling me," said Young Pup. "How can you serve the zoo and not think? How can you be talented and not think? How can alienation be healthy? I don't understand."

The Foxes laughed. They enjoyed Young Pup's blunt honesty. Only in private conversations did one hear honesty in Zooland. The Foxes found it refreshing to see it in Young Pup. Gray Fox said, "Let me try to illustrate. Take for example the Running Dogs of Loyalty. Some of the Running Dogs of Loyalty have talent. They can do their assigned jobs, some with aplomb. But that is really not what gives them satisfaction. What gives them satisfaction is serving the zoo. They are institutional patriots. Pathetically so. They live for the zoo and cannot think outside its roles and duties. They cannot think critically. They cannot question authority."

"Beware," agreed Sly Fox. "They have no selves separate from the zoo. The zoo is their religion, their passion. Most of them actually love their cages. You must be careful what critical thoughts you express in front of a Running Dog of Loyalty. You can be sure he will soon report it to a climbing Baboon. The climbing Baboon will then use it against you in a mounting if it should ever serve his purpose. A Fox never says anything intelligent in front of a Running Dog of Loyalty. Most of them, you see, aspire to be climbing Baboons themselves. A Running Dog is first to squeal."

Said Gray Fox, "The Running Dogs of Loyalty desperately try to fill an inner emptiness with their outward attachments. They need direction. Faith, worship, loyalty, duty, patriotism—these they thoughtlessly consider to be virtues. Because they need order, they attach themselves to those who give orders. They conceive no difference between the zoo and its masters. Unable to think for themselves, Running Dogs of Loyalty always mouth the slogans of order and rank. The zoo is their entire world. Their life. What threatens to upset it, upsets them."

Sly Fox agreed, "Yes. Deviance upsets them. Free thinkers scare them. Rather than question authority, they would clutch Vipers to their breasts. Nothing makes a Running Dog of Loyalty feel better than to see a fellow creature whom he considers disloyal get mounted. It reinforces his longing for order."

"Like Barking Seals, whom they often choose for their friends," added Gray Fox, "Running Dogs of Loyalty occupy a useful niche in the zoo hierarchy. They almost never get mounted. No need. They don't understand their own exploitation. The climbing Baboons simply use them. The climbing Baboons let Running Dogs of

Loyalty roam about the zoo. They send them running errands, doing projects, writing reports, sniffing about for critics and trouble-makers. Watch Dogs and Guard Dogs—ever vigilant for organizational irreverence and rule-breakers." Then he added, "Running Dogs on the loose keep the Rabbits hopping and the Foxes stealthy."

"It would be a lot more pleasant here if someone would put the Running Dogs of Loyalty back in their cages," added Sly Fox with consternation. "It is ironic. You would think the ranking Baboons would like them. They don't. Ranking Baboons actually hold a disdain for them because they are narrow, subservient, obedient. Yet they are useful, so climbing Baboons tolerate them. Even praise them. Beware. Even words of praise may mean the opposite of what they seem."

Gray Fox continued, "What is true regarding Running Dogs of Loyalty is also, in part, true of Barking Seals. Barking Seals are sometimes quite talented. Many work hard; most of them have technical skills. Some are good puzzle-heads. But they are so shallow as to be wholly harmless to climbing Baboons. They simply bark whatever they are told to bark; they do whatever they are told to do; they believe whatever they are told to believe. They follow the troop no matter where it leads. They never ask what is guiding it, where it is going, or why. Their memories are short. They live day-to-day. Like Ants, they revel in zoo gossip. As long as the ranking Baboons occasionally toss them a Fish, the Barking Seals are content. They are completely oblivious to the utter contempt in which they are held by Top Baboon. He pats them on the head and they feel warm inside." After a pause, Gray Fox added, "Those who tend the Sheep, tend to fleece them."

Young Pup asked, "What's the difference, then, between the two?"

"Not much on a practical level," said Sly Fox. "It's
the difference between being narrow-minded and shallow-minded. Running Dogs of Loyalty are narrow.
Barking Seals are shallow. Barking Seals have a fetish for
rules. They love to memorize rules. It gives their petty
minds something to do. Running Dogs of Loyalty, on the
other hand, delight in mindlessly enforcing rules. They
never question by what authority some creatures impose
rules on others.[4]  Neither Barking Seals nor Running
Dogs of Loyalty advance very far."

"True believers comprise the majority of creatures,"[5] said Gray Fox. "A sly Fox must be careful what
he says around narrow- or shallow-minded creatures."
After a pause, he added, "Unlike climbing Baboons, hop-
to-it Rabbits, or we Foxes, Running Dogs of Loyalty and
Barking Seals are not overtly controlled by fear. Since
mountings don't usually happen to them, they really
aren't that directly concerned. Rather, the Running Dogs
of Loyalty and the Barking Seals are motivated by something better, yet twisted. Hope. False hope. Hope—
promises of more Fish, bigger cages with a better view,
higher rank, a slight advantage over their peers here or
there. They desperately suck at the tit of privilege. I
know one Barking Seal who is now content because his
ranking Baboon gave him one half of one percent more
Fish per year than his peers. Ranking Baboons understand this quite well. The zoo always promises far more
than it can ever deliver. For the majority this fraud

works quite well. That their hopes are never realized doesn't matter. It is hoping itself which sustains them. They labor, year after year, on the promise of false hopes. When their hopes come face to face with disappointment, instead of revolting, they settle for crumbs and redouble their hopes. Hope is fraud for the Lamb. Faith is fraud for the Flock. It doesn't matter. Both are futile. An opiate. Hope only screws up your judgment."[6]

He continued, "Look at the pittance which the worker Ants receive! Once a year Top Baboon drops a few Newts to the bottom of the cage. The lowly Ants swarm over it. So do others, like Swine at a trough. By crumbs they foolishly measure themselves, their value, their worth. Most creatures are oblivious of their own oppression. In Zooland, happiness is paid for with self-delusion. As a wise Fox once said, 'Happiness is a perpetual possession of being well deceived.'"[7]

Sly Fox then added, "The zoo—its structure, its hierarchy, its cages—does not allow its creatures to fulfill their natural potentials. Not in the slightest. The small differences in natural talents between creatures cannot justify the obscene differences between their social ranks, rewards, powers, and privileges. Luxury is graft. Wealth is theft.[8] Luxury is stolen from workers by fear and sold back to them as counterfeit hope. A fang and a con. Beware of smiles filled with fangs."

Added Gray Fox, "Look around. The privileged few at the top enjoy vast creature comforts while the many at the bottom sleep on beds of straw. A luxury tax to benefit the rich is built right into the cost of living. The cost of sickness. Even the cost of dying. Every transaction is a theft. Every deal is a steal. Every payday is a payoff—a bribe. A moral reduction. It is no accident. It is structured that way. Do you understand? Every day you live in this zoo you are robbed blind."

Sly Fox said, "Here hypocrisy is palpable. Ranking Baboons do not hesitate to club to death some poor gypsy Rat who, in order to feed his starving family, dares to steal a morsel of food from their dish. At the same time, the Baboons themselves, by rank and power, loot the labor of others, bottom up. Do you see? Petty theft by the poor and helpless is 'crime.' Structured-in theft, on a scale gross and grand, by and for the rich and powerful is 'success.' Such is the ladder of success you are invited to climb." After a pause, he added, "When the gods punish a fool, they grant him his wishes."

Young Pup asked, "How can a creature be oblivious of his own oppression? It doesn't make sense."

Sly Fox answered, "The nature of creatures is to be free.⁹ We are born free yet everywhere we are in chains.¹⁰ Chains shackle us. Bars surround us. Why? When a creature is raised from birth in a cage, the bars of the cage are taken-for-granted as part of reality. The bars become second-nature, a part of one's field of vision. To see the world from behind bars eventually seems natural, taken-for-granted as *a way of life.* Such is the zoo. So you see, the most blatant, oppressive feature of the zoo—its very structure—becomes habitual, invisible. The masses of creatures have eyes, but they cannot see. They have minds, but they cannot think. They have claws, but they cannot fight. Their whole lives are an endless exercise in unquestioned conformity and obedience. A worship of authority. They mouth an allegiance to freedom, while perpetuating the conditions of its denial.[11] They think they are free only because they are not free to think. The chains in their brains deny the chains on their manes. In reality, zoo culture is structured mass self-deception. They do not know any better. Worse. They *cannot* know any better. Look around. Creatures suffer, but they can't think why. Cage amnesia."[12]

"Look at the Gorillas over there," said Gray Fox. "They are truly an exception. Most creatures don't like them. They are always causing problems. They bang and clang against their cages. They even throw their feces at passers-by. Many creatures think they are brain damaged. Gorillas get up in the morning, do their exercises, groom themselves, then go bang their heads against the bars. Day in, day out. In utter futility. Why? There is something inside them longing to be free. They do not conceal it. They do not deny it. Unlike most creatures in the zoo, they have no illusions about the fact they live locked in cages. They know that the zoo is a violation of their nature. They refuse to pretend otherwise. I give them credit. Unlike others, they do not waste their days lacing flowers on their chains."[13] After a pause, Gray Fox added, "Brain-damaged? Yes, those bone-heads are brain-damaged. So what? *Everyone* here is brain-damaged. The zoo is structured that way. But give them credit. They are not as brain-damaged as the self-deluded Baboons who run this place!"

"Be a Fox, not a Gorilla," chuckled Sly Fox. "It is better to grasp structure *in* your head, than *with* it."

Young Pup was beginning to understand. He

asked, "Who becomes a climbing Baboon? Where do they come from?"

Seeing that Young Pup had grasped the issue, if not the process, Sly Fox smiled. "You have asked a good question. I will try to give you an honest answer. Climbing Baboons used to be eager Young Pups like yourself. That's where everyone starts."

"That's right. Remember," interrupted Gray Fox, "no matter how high and mighty a creature may become, he is still a son of a bitch."

Sly Fox continued, "Many of the bright Young Pups then grow into hop-to-it Rabbits. A few of the hop-to-it Rabbits, if they do not first become burned-out Sloths, are promoted to climbing Baboons. Many others become Barking Seals or Running Dogs of Loyalty. A rare few become Foxes. Once a hop-to-it Rabbit is promoted to climbing Baboon, he then becomes increasingly aggressive. Of necessity. The Jackal Principle is half-truth, half-projection. Life in the zoo is Dog-eat-Dog, day in, day out. Look around." After a pause, Sly Fox added, "There are many humorous things in the zoo. Among them is the Baboon notion that he is less savage than other savages.[14] The truth is just the opposite: Life at the top is most savage of all."

Young Pup asked, "But why are so many hop-to-it Rabbits made climbing Baboons?"

"Only a few are chosen. It has to do with their make-up. The hop-to-it Rabbits selected for promotion are chosen because they are neurotic. Efficient, talented, and insecure. They live in perpetual fear of displeasing authority. They have a mortal dread of Top Baboon. They don't like Top Baboon. They don't believe him. They don't trust him. *But they will always obey him.* They therefore can be controlled. Their talents can be marshaled. Top Baboon knows this. These are traits he values. Top Baboon derives great delight in controlling talented others." After a pause, he added, "Power is making others act against their will. Authority is making them unaware of it. Religion is making them happy about it."[15]

"So you see," continued Gray Fox, "contrary to what you were taught in Young Pup School, it is not the most talented who get promoted in Zooland. It is the fear-prone, the compliant, the obedient—these are the prerequisites. If one has talent as well, it is secondary. Unfortunately, some climbing Baboons are quite incompetent and make life miserable for those around them. Few creatures are as psychotic as a neurotic given rank and power. If over-stressed, some climbing Baboons crack. Incompetence is their natural pedigree. Distemper the natural consequence. Do you see? It is structured that way."

Added Sly Fox, "It is true. The fault of our problems today belongs overwhelmingly to incompetent management, yet the blame is cast upon the lowly worker. He who holds the leash always blames the Dog."

Young Pup then asked, "Does a creature that can think but not act have any advantage over a creature that cannot think at all?"

Sly Fox was increasingly impressed with Young Pup. He responded, "That's a foxy question. Some hop-to-it Rabbits and climbing Baboons are not shallow. They can think. It is hard to know how many—just a few. They can think and they can question, but they will not question openly. They will never challenge authority. They are afraid. Fear holds them hostage. Top Baboon knows it. He relies on it. He uses it and they know it. They resent the very hierarchy which, ironically, they daily perpetuate. Even though they inwardly hate the zoo, they serve it just as dutifully as if they loved it. They go along to get along. Neurosis is outer social contradiction manifest as inner conflict. The resolution: You turn into that which you hate." After a pause, Sly Fox added, "Do you understand? Only he who never fears is free."[16]

"Then, why do they go along?" asked Young Pup.

"The zoo is as crooked as a Dog's hind leg. It is structured that way. They know it wrong, but speak it right. Some are caged by fear. Others are stuck in the muck of mendacity," answered Sly Fox. "Either way, they see no exit, no options.[17] Many are old. They are afraid that, if they were to be banished from this zoo, no other zoo would take them in. The zoo is thus structured to promote the thought-compliant. The more neurotic and insecure, the better. The royal road to success is not talent, not courage, not conviction, not integrity, not merit, not independence of thought. It is thought-compliance. Conformity. The way is clear. If you seek success: Make truth foreign to your tongue. Do not let the sufferings of others enter your ears. Say only what masters want to hear. Conform at all costs. Learn how to be trusted to lie.

Never question authority. Be stupid on command. Molt your morals." After a pause, Sly Fox added, "Do you understand? All power is corrupt.[18] Where complicity with power is a virtue, integrity is a vice."

"So," said Young Pup, "the Foxes are thoughtful but not compliant—hence, dangerous to the established order. Running Dogs of Loyalty and Barking Seals are compliant but not thoughtful—hence dangerously narrow or shallow. But the hop-to-it Rabbits, especially those neurotically fearful of authority, are promoted into climbing Baboons because they are both thoughtful and compliant."

"Exactly," said Gray Fox. "A climbing Baboon must fight his rivals, not challenge his superiors. When a climbing Baboon gets too uppity or aggressive nothing pleases a ranking Baboon more than to mount him from behind. One way is to promote a talented, compliant hop-to-it Rabbit into the ranks. The younger the better. This thwarts the climbing Baboon's ambition and deflects his aggressive energies. Top Baboon loves it. 'Divide and conquer' keeps him on top. Perhaps now you understand that the meeting called by Top Baboon was a ritual mounting ceremony. If you think carefully, you will discover that three climbing Baboons, one Fox, three Sloths, two Barnacles, and one Barking Seal got mounted from the rear; two hop-to-it Rabbits and one Running Dog of Loyalty got promoted. Three pension Barnacles got sent out to sea. It is called reorganization. The outworld Jackal Principle and all the rest are just convenient half-truths. A ruse. The zoo is run by Primates on principles unfit for Reptiles."

"Whose interests do you think get served by these endless reorganizations?" said Sly Fox with agitation, "Remember: The most important thing to Top Baboon is that *he* be Top Baboon. The other ranking Baboons, in turn, seek to keep their rank as well. When Top Baboon speaks of loyalty to Zooland he means loyalty to him. Order means his orders. So you see, a reorganization is not a reorganization at all. Just the opposite. It is a savage purge designed to ensure that the structure of Zooland remains exactly the way it is. Power loves power. Power serves power. Nothing else. Ever. To that end, nobody is important, everybody is dispensable." After a pause, he added wryly, "As the Huskie says: If you are not the lead Dog, the scenery never changes."

From a cage nearby came once more the mournful cry of Persian poet Parrot:

When You and I behind the Veil are past,
Oh, but the long long while the World shall last,
　　Which of our Coming and Departure heeds
As much as Ocean of a pebble-cast.

Sly Fox ignored the Bird. He continued, "Words in Zooland mean the opposite of what they mean. The last thing Top Baboon wants is a *real* reorganization. He would be tossed to the Dogs immediately. The rich would be eaten. In reality, the zoo never changes—*you do*. The zoo eats its young. It is structured that way."

"Not a happy thought for a young Pup like me," offered Young Pup. Couplets of an old poem he had learned in Young Pup School echoed in his mind: "...The gay will laugh when thou art gone, the solemn brood of care plod on, and each one as before shall chase his favorite phantom."[19]

Before Young Pup could put them into words, Gray Fox spoke. "A wise old Owl once said, 'Les gens heureux n'ont pas d'histoire.'"[20]

"What does that mean?" asked Young Pup.

"'Happy creatures do not have history.' History is made by unhappy creatures. In days of yore Lions of Truth courageously emerged among the victims of life and led them in revolt," said Gray Fox. "In bygone days it was so. I used to believe in it myself. No more. Unhappy creatures are now as impotent as the rest. And usually as compliant. They are neurotic and impotent. They self-destruct piecemeal or all at once. They cannot make history. Nobody can. History is stalled. History is dead.[21] The zoo is out of options. The Baboons clubbed to death the last of the great Lions of Truth long before we were born. Today there are no Lions of Truth.[22] They live only in myth and legend. We invoke their names but not their notions. It is structured that way. Can you see? The zoo is lie-locked. The zoo never changes." After a pause, he added, "The first half of life is illusionment, the second half is disillusionment."[23]

Young Pup was truly amazed by all this. "I am distressed," he said, "by what you say. It is so negative, so depressing."

Sadness came over Gray Fox. He had been afraid from the start that this might happen. His whiskers drooped. His eyes misted. He walked to the bars of the cage. Wistfully he said, "Oh, Young Pup, if you only

knew what I believed when I was young like you: Sugar
Candy Mountains! Holy Lions, indeed! Love of justice
and love for my fellow creature burned as one in my
brain. Would not the whole world rather hang fast to
the back of a Tiger of Justice than linger as glad fools beneath a sick Elephant's tail? I could not dream it otherwise. I was young. I was wrong. I misjudged how humiliated most creatures are willing to be."

After a pause, he continued, "When I was but a
wee Pup an old pension Barnacle taught me a song
which, he said, in bygone days creatures everywhere used
to sing. It has been lost through the generations. I may
be the last living creature to know it. I don't know. I can
only remember a small part of it. It was a song of hope
and freedom. The pension Barnacle would take me aside
to a place where he could not be overheard and, in little
more than a whisper, he would sing it to me. I remember how, even in his old age, his eyes sparkled when he
sang these verses:[24]

> Rings shall vanish from our noses,
> And the harness from our back,
> Bit and spur shall rust forever,
> Cruel whips no more shall crack.
>
> Riches more than mind can picture,
> Wheat and barley, oats and hay,
> Clover, beans, and mangel-wurzels
> Shall be ours upon that day.
>
> For that day we all must labour,
> Though we die before it break;
> Cows and horses, geese and turkeys,
> All must toil for freedom's sake.

It sounded romantic, even exotic to Young Pup. He liked it and wished he could hear all of it. But he felt a bit embarrassed by Gray Fox's sudden emotions. He wasn't sure how to respond, so he raised a less personal issue. Awkwardly he asked, "How can creatures live in a place where 'they know it to be wrong, but speak it to be right'? Is it possible to live with such internal contradiction? Surely this must have bad consequences."

"Ever hear of Executive Monkeys?" quipped Gray Fox. They all laughed. Then in a serious voice, he asked rhetorically, "Yes, ever hear of ulcers? Of heart attacks? Of strokes? Of nervous breakdowns? Of sexual impotence? Contradictions ultimately rend—first the mind, then the body. A hierarchy motivated by mounting fears from within and fear of Jackals from without is a pathological zoo. In such a badly structured zoo, every situation is caged. The path from one cage leads only to another. The more initiative a creature takes, the greater the blame; the less initiative he takes, the greater the fault. Every choice is a contradiction. The harder one works, less the satisfaction. The less one works, harder the satisfaction.[25] The greater a creature's public success, the greater his personal failure. And so on. Do you understand? A wrong way of life cannot be lived rightly.[26] Eventually the zoo—its contradictions, its pathologies—makes you sick."

"That is why," said Sly Fox, "we Foxes try to stay Foxes. A Fox seldom becomes a climbing Baboon. When climbing Baboons and hop-to-it Rabbits wear down under the stress and strain, they become either burned-out Sloths or pension Barnacles. Some self-destruct. They, too, after all, pay their dues. They pay their dues with their lives. They pay their dues with their lives in a zoo they see cannot be changed. It is structured that way." After a pause, he added, "Where neurosis is a necessity, alienation is a balm."[27]

Young Pup had never heard a creature speak in such a style. It was as if years of life were being condensed into a few sentences. It inspired Young Pup. Boldly, he asked, "Why can't it be changed?"

Swishing his tail against the bars of the cage for emphasis, Gray Fox answered, "Understand. Cages are not just locked. They are *lie-locked*. Physical locks can be picked. Mental locks are much harder. Creatures see that the zoo cannot be changed because they cannot see that it can be changed. A self-fulfilling prophecy. They are not happy. They are not free. They are exploited and victimized at every turn. They learn from bitter experience to trust no one. Often, not even their own love-mates. It is structured that way. It is a loveless, neurotic way of life. Yet, they accept it. Why? Cage amnesia. Structural blindness. Weak brains make strong chains. The masses of creatures are a dead weight.[28] Not even a pride of Lions could rouse them to action."

After a pause, Gray Fox added, "Who by midlife has not tasted the bittersweet need for the eternal triumph of hope over experience?[29] Only by a tremendous capacity to forget pain, is life made tolerable.[30] By young and old alike, there is enough pain and anger and injustice and suffering in this zoo to fuel a dozen revolutions, but not enough intelligence, character, or courage to spark a half-hearted revolt.[31] The mass of creatures lead lives of quiet desperation.[32] The rest live lives of self-delusion. Tomorrow only promises more of the same. Where nothing is worth dying for, nothing is worth living for. If what I say is not the truth, then why do so many Young Pups commit suicide?"

Young Pup was speechless.

Sly Fox elaborated, "The insight in your question, Young Pup, is right: False life damages. Contradictions rend. Life in Zooland cons itself. The structure is overwhelmingly false and yet oppressively real. Any who would scratch the happy-face veneer will find massive amounts of depression. A malicious malaise. Especially among the silent Ants. Why? In Zooland, that which is false is real. That which is true is forbidden. In such a zoo speakers of truth are kept in solitary confinement, banished, or killed. Can you understand? Can you see the rending contradictions?

> Loyalty and truth contradict.
> Hope and experience contradict.
> Intelligence and happiness contradict.
> Integrity and success contradict.
> Self-respect and self-fulfillment contradict.[33]

Damned if you do, damned if you don't. As *a way of life*. It is structured that way. Where the whole is mad, rending contradictions are offered as a normal way of life. In adjusting to the mad whole, the normal creature is made really sick.[34] Look around. Look at the creatures in the zoo: They sleep too much. They eat too much. They drink too much. They gossip too much. They whine too much. They groom too much. They waste too much. They backbite too much. They lie too much. They masturbate too much. They mount each other too much. They kill each other too much. Violence, greed, and fear—day in, day out. Amid all this they rise in the morning, groom their personalities, smile neurotically, and pursue their false happinesses. In this, *as a way of life*, a culture, you are told to take pride. To mouth slogans. To pledge allegiance. Do you understand? You are asked to deny the evidence of your own nose, your own best sense: Cages stink!"

Young Pup was stunned by the blunt truth of what he had heard. Again he was at a loss for words. Sly Fox could see this. After a pause, as if to rest his case, Sly Fox looked at Young Pup and said bluntly, "Welcome to Zooland, Young Pup, where instilling your role means stilling your brain."[35]

After a long pause, Gray Fox spoke. "Young Pup," said Gray Fox with gentleness in his voice, "you are just out of Young Pup School and are young and eager to demonstrate your talents. I know what we have said is hard for you to understand. Hard on your optimistic view of life. Hard on the pablum of common-sense fed you since birth. But I make no excuses. I do not hide the fact that I seek your disillusionment. I pluck the flowers from your chains that you might know what others don't: *the difference*. You asked for it by being bright. Here, narrow-mindedness is a virtue, a well-rounded intelligence is a curse. You are cursed. Try to understand. You think that you have come here to learn, to demonstrate what you know and can do. No. The goal of the Baboons is to teach you what you can't do. Prepare to unlearn more than you learn.

"Sooner or later you will recognize that we are not pessimists. We are not cynics. We are just Foxes. Honest Foxes—willing to share with you honest reflections on a magical zoo. Sooner or later you must grow up. You must leave your Puppyhood and its Puppy loves behind. We simply warn you that it can be painful. You should know the source of the pain. It is this. You will *have* to make choices among rending contradictions. Between torn choices. Sly Fox named them. I will not repeat them. What you choose determines what you are. A Barking Seal. A Fox. A climbing Baboon. And so on. The point is this. You cannot win. You cannot escape. Your life will be damaged. Your brain will be stained." After a pause, Gray Fox add, "Beneath the skin of every cynic lies a heart-broken idealist."

Sly Fox added, "It is true. Most creatures do this without reflection. They cannot conceive the whole. They live piecemeal, blind as a Bat. As they move along the course of life day-by-day the only sense they have that they are changed by large and contradictory forces is the melancholy discovery that they made promises which they can no longer keep. They break their vows but don't know why. They feel themselves torn apart but can't comprehend why. Their identities are broken into pieces. Their lives are lived in fragments. They see only the day ahead. For relief, they hug a joy that's cheap.[36] They are divorced from themselves. They glimpse the whole only fleetingly, with their fuzzy emotions, not with mental clarity. In the end, their lives are one long regret. Can you see? Cage amnesia distorts a full grasp of reality. To veil truth from the mind robs the heart. Without truth, the pursuit of joy ends joylessly." After a pause, he added, "The truth is this: The zoo relies upon your stupidity more than your intelligence."

Came the melancholy cry of Persian poet Parrot:

Into this Universe, and why not knowing,
Nor whence, like Water willy-nilly flowing;
And out of it, as Wind along the Waste,
I know not whither, willy-nilly blowing.

Young Pup asked, "How do such creatures deal with that which is greater than themselves—that which they can feel but not comprehend?"

Sly Fox answered, "The mystified mystify. The petrified petrify. Those who cannot grasp social force— the whole—in reality *as* reality, abstract, mystify, and petrify it. They make it supernatural, mystical, holy. They deify it. The whole—that which they can feel in their lives, yet cannot comprehend in their brains—they make deity. Holy Lions. Mythical saviors. There is a deep and sad irony in their attempt to petrify emotional understanding, especially as distorted by cage amnesia. By cutting off their divine inventions from reality— from the actual historical conditions of misery and damage which give rise to them in the first place[37]—they make the whole worse than it already is. Isn't the zoo bad enough already? Isn't the zoo oppressive enough without creatures endlessly judging, damning, attacking, and killing each other in the name of their holy fabrications? Do you understand? A false cure worsens a bad disease." After a pause, he added softly, "Indeed, woe is the eternal mother of self-pity. The best medicine for misery is neither myth nor miracle, but naked truth."

"Sad irony, indeed," said Gray Fox. "False premises always lead to false promises.[38] Mysticism re-damages the already damaged.[39] It afflicts the afflicted. It blames the victim for his life-inflicted sense of guilt and stain. Blind to social structure, the hapless victim blames himself. Do you understand? You shall be expected, day in and day out, life-long, to forfeit your brain. Once you forfeit your brain, whether for gains *social or spiritual*, you enter the perfect cage: Your own head. The iron cage around you becomes a repressive cage within you.[40] You may think analytically, but never again *critically*. And this they call liberation! Salvation! Beware. Words often mean the opposite of what they mean. Beware of promises of life which have death as a prerequisite."

Woefully cried Persian poet Parrot:

Oh, threats of Hell and Hopes of Paradise!
One thing at least is certain—This Life flies;
One thing is certain and the rest is Lies;
The Flower that once is blown forever dies.

Young Pup was amazed at the sagacious Parrot. Again the Foxes ignored the Bird. Sly Fox said, "Who can bear the whips and scorns of time?[41] Growing old is not for prissy Poodles. The true reasons for faith are earthy, indeed. All of them, including self-pity and guilt, are melancholic. The worship of religion is the worship of society—unknowingly—by the broken-headed and broken-hearted. In reality, the sacred is the profane made invisible to itself.[42] Nothing more than this: A worship of our fathers, conceived without flesh. Look around. There are as many religions as there are species. Yet religion is everywhere the same. It is the sigh of the oppressed creature, the sentiment of a heartless zoo, the hope of the hopeless. Religion is the opiate of the masses.[43] If—in a proper sense—there were no chains, no cages, no whips and scorns, then there would be no need to invent otherworldly escapes. Supernaturalism is the false hope of escape, of justice, of something better, clutched in desperation by the spirit-broken, the life-damaged, the tired-of-being-kicked, the never-had-a-chance, the born-to-lose, the suffers-too-much, and the soon-to-die. Running Dogs of Loyalty, Barking Seals, and very Young Pups—the narrow, the shallow, and the innocent—are obvious candidates, too."

Young Pup's ears stood straight up.

Sly Fox continued, "I teach you two truths, one hard and one sad: The hard truth is this. We cannot escape from this zoo. It is structured that way. And no supernatural Lion is going to appear out of nowhere to save us. Ever. For better or worse, full responsibility for our condition and our fate is ours and ours alone.[44] Life in this zoo has no meaning except that meaning which we ourselves give it.[45] We and we alone must choose between the kingdom and the darkness.[46]

"The sad truth is this: Not five creatures in a hundred can bear to face the hard truth. They are not mature. They want to live by wishing, clinging to the emotional errors and conceptual mistakes left over from Puppyhood. They shirk responsibility for our condition and our future by projecting it onto supernatural scapegoats. Most creatures prefer a warm lie to a cold truth. If you make them feel good, the masses will love you. If you make them think, they will hate you. I warn you: He who dares disturb the sleepwalk of masses, prepares for nightmare. Can you see? The persistence of religion across the generations is a double proof: Life in the zoo is not bearable honestly and is honestly unbearable. Sweet lies are born to hide bitter truths."

Added Gray Fox, "Each creature clings to the fantasy of a happy ending. There are no happy endings. Just melodrama in the meantime. All relationships end in separation. All. The rest is illusion and denial." After a pause, he added, "You can't fool reality, only yourself."

Again came the haunting cry of Persian poet Parrot:

The Moving Finger writes; and, having writ,
Moves on: nor all your Piety nor Wit
Shall lure it back to cancel half a Line,
Nor all your Tears wash out a Word of it.

"Amazing Bird!" thought Young Pup to himself.

Sly Fox ignored the Bird, adding, "Beware of Running Dogs of Loyalty—True Believers—who self-righteously foam at the mouth. The mentally stunted turn morally rabid. In their souls, the Running Dogs of Loyalty are mad. They will kill on command. And enjoy it. I shall tell you a truth which, at your innocent age, you cannot believe: Most creatures do not seek to escape to freedom. They seek to escape from freedom.[47] Why? So much have they come, twisted by life, to enjoy the gains from illness. Gains from illness nurse their self-delusions."[48]

"What illness?" asked Young Pup.

"Guilt," replied Sly Fox.

"Guilt? A gain from guilt?" puzzled Young Pup.

"Oh, yes," answered Sly Fox. "Guilt is pains re-membered, fears approved, and humiliations accept-ed—all in one—the ugliest, yet most effective of all men-tal chains. The mass of creatures do not hate guilt. They enjoy it. They depend on it for guidance. Like a voice, it tells them what to do and what not to do. Whom to like and whom to shun. It spares them having to think for themselves. Better even than whips, guilt ensures obedi-ence to authority. Those stained by guilt are always the enemy of freedom. Always an ally of authority. Free thinkers terrify them. They *want* authority to father over them. They *want* their cages. They *want* surrogate fathers to tell them what to do. By the time they reach adulthood, their brains are dead on arrival. Their imagi-nations are imaginary. Do not waste your time debating the close-minded. They cannot understand you. Their repressions will not allow it." After a pause, Sly Fox added, "As a sharp old Eagle once said, 'Loyalty to petri-fied opinions never yet broke a chain or freed a single creature in *this* world—and never will.'"[49]

"'Their imaginations are imaginary.' How can you tell?" asked Young Pup.

"Easy," responded Sly Fox. "The guilt-sated make endless apologies for things as they are. They make end-less excuses for the vanities, stupidities, and crimes of au-thority. To them, authority is right, no matter what. Some are so ignorant that they actually believe the rich should be rich, the powerful should be powerful, and the poor should be poor. The thought of revolution strikes fear in their hearts and diarrhea in their bowels. The rabid voice of guilt speaks clearly: Say 'law and order.' Mean order. Say 'liberty.' Mean security. Say 'freedom of speech.' Mean freedom from thought. Say 'reform.' Mean status quo. Say 'individualism.' Mean conformity. Say 'morality.' Mean power. Say 'equality.' Mean inequality. Say 'justice.' Mean injustice. Alas, now you know the secret heartbeat of Zooland, the root of all its crippling pathologies—repressive guilt." After a pause, Sly Fox added, "A wise old Fox, long ago, put it best: 'Conscience doth make cowards of us all.'"[50]

Gray Fox interrupted, pointing with his paw, "Speaking of Running Dogs of Loyalty, here comes one now. Brother Canine."

Sly Fox spied him instantly. "Young Pup, let me do the talking," said Sly Fox as he walked to the bars of the cage.

Running Dog of Loyalty trotted up to the cage, careful not to poke his nose through the bars as Running Dogs have been known to get clawed on the snout. "Hail, Brothers. How are we today?" said Running Dog. "And howls our young Pup getting along?" He chuckled at his own pun as he glanced condescendingly toward Young Pup. "We are new here, aren't we?" he said to Young Pup, not wanting an answer. Young Pup noticed that those in authority use the word "we" whenever possible. "Pack mentality," he thought to himself.

Sly Fox sat down on his haunches. "I and my companions were discussing the new zoo initiatives outlined this morning. Tell me, Brother Canine, why do you make tracks here?" asked Sly Fox.

"Well, we have a message. The Office of the Assistant to Top Baboon has announced that important visitors will be coming to visit the zoo tomorrow. Among them will be dignitaries from the Canine Intelligence Agency. Top Baboon wants us—our accommodations—to look their best. We all know appearances are very important. Perception is reality. Every creature sports a feature. To groom is to bloom. Good work is teamwork," preached Brother Canine, reciting Zooland slogans. "We request that you..."

"You mean you *order* the usual 'suggestions'?" interrupted Sly Fox, with sarcasm in his voice.

Brother Canine knew it was futile to try to out fox a Fox. "That's right," he said with a sense of authority, dropping all pretense. "The order," he said brazenly, "is for us to be well groomed. Our accommodations must be clean. No pissing on the straw. No napping. We must be alert and friendly. Of course, all bowls will be filled with food and must be left uneaten until our guests have gone. Howling, barking, or whimpering is forbidden. Do we have any questions?"

Sly Fox answered mockingly, yet in a cooperative tone, "No. We understand. Please tell Top Baboon that he may rest assured we will waste no time implementing his suggestions."

Gray Fox, his sleek gray sheen blending with the shadows of evening light, glanced quickly at Young Pup to see if... He had. At that moment Young Pup let out a yelp of laughter.

"What's the matter with him?" snapped Running Dog of Loyalty. Sly Fox deflected the question. He said calmly, "We will certainly give your instructions the attention they deserve. You may count on that."

Young Pup, now a bit fearful, suppressed his impulse to laugh aloud again. "Good," said Running Dog of Loyalty. "We know we can count on you. We must be going. Cat Division next—whiskered beasts! Good to see you, Brother Canines. You, too, Young Pup." For sport he raised his hind leg and feigned to piss in Young Pup's direction. He laughed when Young Pup drew back. Having done his duty, Running Dog of Loyalty trotted happily away to other cages.

Young Pup felt humiliated. It hurt. He took the only revenge he could. "He didn't get it, did he!" exclaimed Young Pup derisively.

Gray Fox tried to help Young Pup recover his dignity. "Everybody's got a cousin or two they ought to be ashamed of," mused Gray Fox apologetically. "Unfortunately, he's ours."

"Someone should box that Cur's arrogant ears," growled Sly Fox. "Imagine a flea-bitten son-of-a-bitch like that giving orders to a Fox! What a zoo!"

After a long silence, as if to let Sly Fox calm down, Gray Fox turned to Young Pup and said softly, "Words are but the film on deep water.[51] You are cursed to peer more deeply into things. There is an understanding gained only in the school of experience. Sooner or later you will recognize that the whole zoo, *as a way of life*, is false.[52]

You may even be surprised to know that many of the ranking Baboons know it and will confess it in private. It may take you years to see the truth of what we say. It may take you a lifetime. It may not be until you are well on your way to Slothhood. Or when you are a pension Barnacle put out to sea. But when you come to realize that the whole is false, you will then understand why speakers of truth are unwelcome, scorned, even killed. Where falsehood reigns, truth of necessity appears as negative. Truth is now shunned as a Snake. Can you see? Today truth has become intolerable. Truth is taboo. Today, all public communication is of domination, by domination, and for domination."[53]

Sadly called out Persian poet Parrot:

Ah, Love! could you and I with Fate conspire
To grasp this sorry Scheme of Things entire,
    Would not we shatter it to bits—
and then Re-mold it nearer to the Heart's Desire!

Sly Fox turned toward the Bird. "Parrot, you speak the truth," said Sly Fox in an unusually mellow, resigned voice. "Oh, what anguish to be wise where wisdom is a loss."[54] His sleek fur glowed orange in the evening sun. Turning to Young Pup, he said, "Do you have the intellectual courage, Young Pup, to penetrate this Spider web of self-masking, interlocking lies, both social and spiritual? To say in your mind: A pox on both of your cages! Then, lest you be killed, to keep this truth to yourself? It is not always easy to unmask lies. But it is always dangerous. To do so, you must be a Fox. It is one of the burdens of Foxhood to keep truth caged in one's own mind, under arrest, in order to save it from being altogether exiled. If truth and sanity are ever to have a chance, the negative must be saved.[55] Regardless of the compromises forced upon you, when given the choice between the lesser of two evils, say in your heart: I choose neither. A pox on both of you!"[56] After a pause, he added, "Here, only the dead dare tell the truth.[57] But who will listen to their silent cries?"

"In Zooland, you see," said Gray Fox, "all choices are wrong. Life is caged on all sides. It is structured that way. If we appear negative, it is because the truth is a danger. Public condemnation is the price an honest creature pays for his integrity in the midst of a corrupt whole. If honesty makes one offensive, then one should be happy to offend deeply. If truth makes one negative, then one should rejoice in being as negative as hell." He quickly added, "But don't! Don't do it! If you insult those in power with protestations of truth, if you unmask their half-truths and lies, your leash on life will be cut short. Life will be choked out of you as if by a slowly twisting chain. Don't be naive. They know how. They have a muzzle fit for every snout. Your bowl will be empty. In the end, the Running Dogs of Loyalty—a cult of faith and force—will slit your throat. If need be, they will not hesitate to burn you and your wee ones alive." After a long pause he added, "Listen well. Where hunger holds courage hostage, fate schools the masses in the Ethics of Cowardice."

Sly Fox was agitated. He stood up and walked in a wide arc. His ears were twitching. "The Ethics of Cowardice!" he snorted. "The whole zoo is filling up with Tickbirds! Tinamou! Ostriches! Their Lice and Fleas. Parasites all!" He then stopped in front of Young Pup and sat back on his haunches. With sparks in his eyes, Sly Fox looked at Young Pup, "The most important thing I can tell you is this: *Grasp structure whole.* If you don't, you will simply be jerked around, mounted, used, and discarded. How? Beware the twin fangs of the sacred and the profane. One is faith and one is force. The spiritual world rests upon faith. The social world rests upon force. Both are poisonous. Look around. Faith and force are the twin destroyers of the world.[58] Piety and power work in concert: What one falsely promises the other falsely redeems. Do you understand? A creature who is truly free has no need of faith and no use for force. His only request is to be judged by merit—to live and let live.

"Is it not transparent? The dish of life is empty. What you see all about you, day in, day out—all that we have hinted at here today—are the decaying forms of a whole which, as a way of life, is morally barren. What was once a vibrant community of freedom-loving creatures has collapsed from within: Patriotically mystified. Organizationally petrified. Individually stultified. It is now a zoo, a smelly zoo. The creed of greed has bred its breed: *Baboons* have taken over. Disgusting creatures! Aggressive, self-seeking, vain, blinded by their assumptions. They lack the Lynx-eyed vision to foresee that they themselves shall be lashed by the lessons of their fraud[59] —the self-destruction which their shallow ethics ensures. The zoo is out of options. It is not honest. It survives by secrecy, deceit, and endless denials. The Lions of Truth are turning in their graves. Will the zoo last many more generations? The symptoms are everywhere—the clearest of which is the denial of symptoms: 'Don't think, believe.' Today, in desperation, the fangs of faith and force are frenetically called upon to inject life into a decaying corpse. Piety made secular is patriotism. Power made holy is duty. Patriotism and religion are morally incestuous. Either way, the cure is the disease. Do you understand? A badly wounded Snake will bite itself. Such is the deep, ultimate irony of cage amnesia."

Young Pup did not understand these words, but sensed their importance to the Foxes who had befriended him. "What will happen to us? What will become of the zoo?" asked Young Pup anxiously. "Do zoos have a life-cycle, too?"

Ruefully cried Persian poet Parrot:

One Moment in Annihilation's Waste,
One Moment, of the Well of Life to taste—
    The Stars are setting, and the Caravan
Draws to the Dawn of Nothing—Oh, make haste!

Sly Fox said, "Organizations are like Fish. The head rots first. Look around. Leaders mask the malevolence of their rank and deeds with mendacity and arrogance—preludes to madness. Mad dragons swallow their own tails. Zoos do not quietly die of old age, they commit suicide, they self-destruct. Look around. Long ago a wise Fox once said, 'Whom the Holy Lions devour...'"[60]

Gray Fox interrupted abruptly, speaking in a foreign tongue intended to conceal his thought from Young Pup, "Das Beste, was du wissen kannst, darfst du den Buben doch nicht sagen."[61] ["One's deepest insights may not be shared with children."]

Sly Fox looked at Gray Fox. He understood the reason for Gray Fox's request. He answered, "Wovon man

nicht sprechen kann, darüber muss man schweigen."[62]
["That which we cannot speak about, we must pass over
in silence."]

Gray Fox nodded his agreement. He turned to
Young Pup and said matter-of-factly, "As for the individ-
ual? As a wise Fox said long, long ago, 'Of these now am
I also one: An exile from god and a wanderer, having
put my trust in raging strife.'[63] That should suffice for
any honest creature worthy of the name." After a pause,
he added, "And as for the zoo? Tell me. When does an
ark of hope become a ship of fools?[64] Answer: When
one can no longer tell the difference. Look around. You
decide."

Gray Fox then swung his nose toward the setting
sun and sniffed the air. He said to Sly Fox, "The air
smells damp. Perhaps it will rain tonight. The Zebras
are still. They are often still before a good rain."

Sly Fox responded, "Let us hope. Rain is always
welcome in a zoo. It settles the creatures like nothing
else. Even the Birds. A moment of peace. A respite
when all are still. A cool rain lifts the burden of heat.
Fresh air clears away the smell for awhile." Turning to
Young Pup, he said, "Young Pup, I like you. I thank you
for listening patiently to a couple of old Foxes. But you
are not ready for the answer to your question. Your
whiskers are too short. You have no context for understanding the answer. Not yet. Perhaps we will talk
again."

Gray Fox walked across the cage and stared sympa-
thetically toward Persian poet Parrot. Except for the ran-

dom wink of one eye, Persian poet Parrot perched with majestic motionlessness. Silent. Addressing him, Gray Fox said, "You understand, don't you, you wise old Cager, you. What a pathetic place: Our leaders are liars while the truth is for the Birds." Turning to Young Pup, he said, "Can you see? It is structured that way."

The two Foxes fell somber and silent. Evening had come. The bars of the cage cast long, widening shadows across the floor. The chatter of the zoo gradually subsided. All the creatures in Zooland were quiet except for the last repining call of Persian poet Parrot from a cage nearby:

'Tis all a Chequer-board of Nights and Days
Where Destiny with Us for Pieces plays:
    Hither and thither moves, and mates, and slays,
And one by one back in our Closet lays.

The Parrot's anthem laden dusk with a heavy sadness. As if seeing them for the first time, Young Pup turned and stared sullenly at the bars of the cage. Strangely, they looked different. A fury he had never felt before welled up inside his breast. A knot choked in his throat. His brain throbbed. He turned his face away from the others. A tear spilled out of his wide eyes and down his face. He said nothing aloud, but in his heart he vowed, "I shall escape!"

The purple and gray colors of twilight melted, leaving the creatures of Zooland in sticky blackness. Gray Fox thought to himself, "I know what you are thinking, Young Pup. I am so sorry...so sorry..."

The three creatures lay still. Finally, Sly Fox mur-

mured softly in the darkness as if in a dream, "I wish I were a Lion."

To sooth the ache of his troubled friend, Gray Fox softly recited his ancient refrain:  "'Rings shall vanish from our noses, and the harness from our back...'" Softer still, Young Pup picked up the rhyme, "'Bit and spur shall rust forever, cruel whips no more shall crack.'" Gray Fox was pleasantly surprised. He smiled in the darkness. Then Sly Fox gently whispered, "'Though we die before it break, all must toil for freedom's sake.'" No one spoke. The two Foxes and Young Pup each curled up and, using his paw for a pillow, wrapped his tail about him and went to sleep in a cage in Zooland. A gentle rain began to fall.

# Chapter Three

## The Next Day

---

Long before daylight the Birds were all a chatter. Persian poet Parrot was gone. The door to his cage stood wide open. Not a feather was found. He had not been eaten. Worse than murder, someone had set him free. Officially, of course, the crime was "First degree Birdnapping."

At dawn a rumor swept through the zoo that a Lion of Truth had been seen lurking nearby. Gypsy Rats from the outworld said they had seen Lion of Truth tracks. The Running Dogs of Loyalty went on full alert. Top Dog at the Canine Intelligence Agency called the Lion of Truth rumor, "Hogwash." With accidental candor, he reassured everybody, "It couldn't be true. After all, there hasn't been a speaker of truth in Zooland for generations."

It was a terrible slip. Ranking Baboons took it as an insult. A furor erupted between ranking Baboons and Running Dogs of Loyalty at the CIA. Ranking Baboons called for Top Dog's removal. One called him "an ignorant son of a bitch." Wild Boars in the Swine Division said he "didn't know Hogwash from Dog shit" and cried "Racist!" Legal Pigs squealed "defamation of character." When Top Dog called the accusations "Bullshit," the Bovine Division joined the fray. Then a climbing Baboon called Top Dog "a Horse's ass." The Zebras vowed to hunger strike.

Top Dog responded incoherently. "I never said the masses are Asses," whined Top Dog. "I said the Asses are massive." The whole Equine Division stampeded. Gazelles and Impalas trampled two Baboons to death and seriously injured four others. Zooland was suddenly turmoil.

To squelch the rumor, CIA Dogs began an immediate dragnet. The Cats denied that they had started the rumor. The Birds denied that they had spread it. The nervous hop-to-it Rabbits denied that they had even heard it. The Gorillas denied that they cared, one way or the other. They all lied. Of course, pleading innocent when guilty was routine behavior in Zooland. The ranking Baboons, of course, were not interrogated.

"Who would dare to set the Bird free?" creatures wondered. "Who would want to be!" answered the dumbfounded. Conspiracy theories were rampant. Some said the ranking Baboons did it to embarrass the CIA. Others said the opposite. Ranking Baboons, of course, saw to it that rumor-mongers savagely slandered Persian poet Parrot: "Bird-brain," "radical," "Parrot-face," "trouble-maker," "traitor," "hook nose," "feather head," "disgruntled misfit," and so on.

Running Dogs of Loyalty—jaws set, eyes glazed, fangs dripping saliva—roamed about in a frenzy. Barking Seals were alternately giddy and petrified. One panic-stricken Barking Seal suffered a nervous breakdown. He barked 20 times, "The end of the world is come. Savior Seal is near to shore," then fell over on his nose in a catatonic fit. A pack of Running Dogs of Loyalty mobbed him: "He released the Parrot—an obvious act of madness." They tore him to pieces and drank his blood.

Just beyond the zoo, a creature tauntingly shot through the underbrush as if to ignite the leaves. In hot pursuit, Brother Canine, the Running Dog of Loyalty, zealously ran circles around the perimeter of the zoo. At noon his heart burst. He died as he had wished—serving the zoo and foaming at the mouth. Outworld Jackals and gypsy Rats ate his carcass. Amid the turmoil, the puzzling question, "What was he chasing?" was never even asked.

The ranking Baboons, with great embarrassment, canceled the visitation schedule for the zoo. In mid afternoon, upon orders from Top Baboon, all the creatures assembled.

"You sons of bitches," he began, "the zoo is not right..." The Barking Seals and Running Dogs of Loyalty in attendance all sat at attention. Of course, they always sat at attention when Top Baboon spoke. Top Baboon was well groomed. He spoke eloquently of the virtue of "team players," the vice of "disloyalty," and the "sacred duty of all creatures to their fellow creatures during an emergency." He eulogized Brother Canine. Top Baboon revealed that Brother Canine had been a secret agent of the CIA and awarded him a posthumous promotion. A Bone Fund for Outstandingly Obedient Puppies was established in his name. Trained Seals gave a 21-bark salute.

Top Baboon announced that ranking Baboon No. 2

would form a Select Committee on Unzooian Activities to ferret out organizational Moles, Rats, Weasels, and Skunks. The Barking Seals all clapped. Of course, Barking Seals always applauded whatever Top Baboon said. They were joined by the Running Dogs of Loyalty and, of course, the ranking Baboons.

The two Foxes sat as expressionless as old Sloths. They said nothing to anyone. They pretended to listen to Top Baboon. Gray Fox's eyes sparkled like the eyes of the old Barnacle who had taught him heroic rhymes when he was but a wee Pup. Sly Fox, too, heard nothing that Top Baboon said. One sentence danced happily through his brain: "He who never fears is free." Young Pup was missing.

After the meeting the two Foxes returned to their cage. They were startled by what they found—in broad daylight! A message. They quickly read it, then Gray Fox erased the evidence with his tail. In the dust were brazenly written the ancient words of a Lion of Truth:[65]

God forbid we should ever be 20 springs without rebellion. What community can preserve its liberties if its rulers are not warned from time to time that creatures preserve the spirit of resistance? Let every creature bare fang and claw. What significance is it if a few lives are lost in a century or two? The tree of liberty must be refreshed from time to time with the blood of patriots and tyrants. It is its natural manure.

We who are about to live, Salute You!
—Outlaws on the Ridge.

Life, it seemed, held potential after all.

# Notes

---

*All truly wise thoughts have been
thought already thousands of times; but
to make them truly ours, we must think
them over again honestly, till they take
root in our personal experience.*

—*Johann Wolfgang Goethe*
*1749-1832*

All passages recited by Persian poet Parrot are select qua-
trains from the *Rubaiyat of Omar: Khayyam* as translated
into English by Edward Fitzgerald in 1859 (Doubleday &
Company, Inc., Garden City, New York). Several transla-
tions were consulted. Omar Khayyam's date of birth is
unknown; he died about 1123.

In using quoted materials, minor poetic license has been
exercised to accommodate the allegorical genre. The
views expressed are solely those of the animals and do
not represent any human beings or their organizations.
Recall, however, that words in Zooland often mean the
opposite of what they mean.

1. Henry David Thoreau, 1817-1862.
2. Heraclitus, 6th-5th century B.C.
3. Sigmund Freud, 1856-1939. *Civilization and Its Discontents.*
4. Max Weber, 1864-1920.
5. Eric Hoffer, 1902-1983.
6. Don Fehr, baseball union negotiator, August, 1994.
7. Jonathan Swift, 1667-1745. *The Tale of the Tub.*
8. Pierre Joseph Proudhon, 1809-1865.
9. Jean-Paul Sartre, 1905-1980.
10. Jean Jacques Rousseau, 1712-1778.
11. Russell Jacoby, 1945- . *Social Amnesia,* 1975.
12. Russell Jacoby. Sigmund Freud. See concept of repression.
13. Karl Marx, 1818-1883. The flower-chain metaphor is used elsewhere as well.
14. Mark Twain, 1835-1910. "There are many humorous things in the world, among them is the white man's notion that he is less savage than other savages."
15. Max Weber.
16. Chippewa Indian saying taught their children in the story "Shingebiss."
17. Jean-Paul Sartre.
18. John Acton, 1834-1902.
19. William Cullen Bryant, 1794-1878. *Thanatopsis.*
20. An old French proverb.
21. Francis Fukuyama, *The End of History and the Last Man,* 1993.
22. Friedrich Nietzsche, 1844-1900.
23. Mark Twain. "The man who is a pessimist before forty-eight knows too much; if he is an optimist after it, he knows too little."
24. George Orwell, 1903-1950. *Animal Farm.*

25. Karl Marx.
26. Theodor Adorno, 1903-1969.
27. Sigmund Freud.
28. Karl Marx.
29. This phrase adapted from Samuel Johnson, 1709-1784.
30. Margaret Mead, 1901-1978.
31. Judy Henderson. "Emotions and the Left."
32. Henry David Thoreau.
33. Russell Jacoby.
34. Theodor Adorno.
35. Russell Jacoby.
36. Sophocles, 496?-406 B.C. *Antigone*.
37. Karl Marx.
38. Robert B. Sipe. "False Premises, False Promises: A Re-Examination of the Human Potential Movement."
39. Nathaniel Branden, 1930- . "Mental Health versus Mysticism and Self-Sacrifice," 1963.
40. Max Weber. "Iron cage" was Weber's metaphor of modern bureaucracy.
41. William Shakespeare, 1564-1616.
42. Emile Durkheim, 1858-1917.
43. Karl Marx.
44. Jacques Monod, 1910-1976. *Chance and Necessity*, 1971.
45. Erich Fromm, 1900-1980.
46. Jacques Monod.
47. Erich Fromm.
48. Sigmund Freud. "The Common Neurotic State," 1917.
49. Mark Twain. "Consistency," 1885.
50. Shakespeare.

51. Ludwig Wittgenstein, 1889-1951.

52. Theodor Adorno.

53. Jurgen Habermas, 1929-    . *Knowledge and Human Interests,* 1968.

54. Sophocles. *Oedipus Rex.*

55. Jean-Paul Sartre; Theodor Adorno; Herbert Marcuse, 1898-1979.

56. Karl Krause, 1874-1936.

57. Mark Twain. "...only dead men can tell the truth in this world."

58. Ayn Rand, 1905-1982. *Philosophy: Who Needs It,* 1982.

59. Sophocles. *Oedipus Rex.*

60. "Whom the gods destroy they first make mad." Euripides, 480?-406 B.C.

61. Literally: "The best that thou canst know thou mayst not tell to boys." Goethe, 1749-1832. *Faust,* Part I, Scene 4.

62. Ludwig Wittgenstein. *Tractatus Logico-Philosophicus.* 7.0.

63. Empedocles, 490-430 B.C.

64. "Ark of hope" was Thomas Jefferson's metaphor for the United States of America.

65. Thomas Jefferson, 1743-1826. "God forbid we should ever be 20 years without such a rebellion... What country can preserve its liberties if its rulers are not warned from time to time that this people preserve the spirit of resistance? Let them take arms... What signify a few lives lost in a century or two? The tree of liberty must be refreshed from time to time with the blood of patriots & tyrants. It is its natural manure." [Letter to Colonel William S. Smith in 1787].

\* \* \* \* \* \* \* \*